Super Smutty
SIGN LANGUAGE

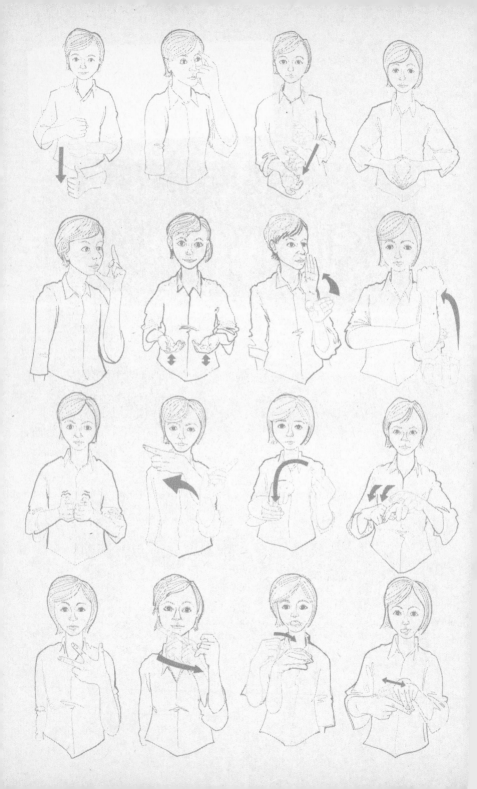

Super Smutty
SIGN LANGUAGE

Kristin Henson

Illustrations by Herb Shaw

ST. MARTIN'S GRIFFIN   NEW YORK

SUPER SMUTTY SIGN LANGUAGE. Copyright © 2013 by Kristin Henson. All rights reserved. Printed in the United States of America. For information, address St. Martin's Press, 175 Fifth Avenue, New York, N.Y. 10010.

www.stmartins.com

Library of Congress Cataloging-in-Publication Data

Henson, Kristin
  Super smutty sign language / Kristin Henson ; illustrations by Herb Shaw.—
First Edition.
    pp. cm.
  ISBN 978-1-250-02621-7 (trade paperback)
  ISBN 978-1-250-03649-0 (e-book)
1. Sign language. 2. English language—Obscene words. I. Title.
  HV2474.H46 2013
  419'.7081—dc23

                                        2013015014

St. Martin's Griffin books may be purchased for educational, business, or pro-motional use. For information on bulk purchases, please contact Macmillan Corporate and Premium Sales Department at 1-800-221-7945, extension 5442, or write specialmarkets@macmillan.com.

First edition: October 2013

10 9 8 7 6 5 4 3 2 1

For my two main men, Greg and Jake

CONTENTS

ACKNOWLEDGMENTS

It takes a village to make a book happen, and by no account did I make this journey alone. The following people deserve much more than a mention on an acknowledgments page, but it's at least a good start.

My parents have awesome senses of humor and were completely supportive when I called to meekly tell them they might hear about their daughter and her dirty sign language. They were even more supportive when I called to tell them I was writing a book. Thank you so much, Mom and Dad, for everything.

Special thanks to Greg, who has been my rock throughout all of this. He's helped with countless tasks, from taking photos for illustrations to giving me suggestions for new phrases. His encouragement has largely been the foundation for this book, and he's kept me sane throughout the process.

I'd like to give a huge thank-you to my interpreting consultant, Matthew. Although most of the words and phrases I asked him about were much, much dirtier than his regular vocabulary, he was always great at getting across the concepts I needed. Thanks for lending your incredible talent to this project. Another interpreter more worthy of any mention I could give here is C.E. She started helping me out and tutoring me, and has taught me more than I ever thought possible about parameters, classifiers, nonmanual markers, and topicalization. I'm so glad I've gained you as a friend and mentor.

My literary agents, Jean and Alison; my editor, Daniela; and my illustrator, Herb, have all been absolutely incredible throughout all of this. All of you ladies have left me with the impression that the publishing industry is filled with intelligent, good-humored, confident women, and I've really appreciated being a part of it for a short bit. I was extremely lucky that Jean happened to stumble across my YouTube channel, and reached out to me. Thank you so much for believing in me, and helping to explain everything along the way.

Among the Deaf community, I'd really like to thank my friends Alex, David, and Brian, and also Julie, Carlisle, Tom, Jordan, and Richard. Your support has meant a lot to me, and I've really appreciated your insight and kind words. I'd also like to thank my ASL teachers Heather and Kaitlyn, as they've been instrumental in my growth.

Thank you to my friends Duncan and Kara, who provided help with any legal jargon I encountered and never yelled at me for making them mute the television numerous times to record a new video, even if it was in the middle of a really good sports game.

Other thanks: Lee Brumbaugh! (who is awesome), Jake and Scarlett (who are cats), and Pete (also a cat).

And of course, thanks go to Lee and Paul and Frank, for the spark that started the YouTube channel.

INTRODUCTION

Hi there! My name's Kristin. I started learning American Sign Language (ASL) in college, when a friend jokingly taught me a few dirty signs instead of the innocuous words I had asked him for. Ever since, I've been trying to learn as much about sign language and Deaf culture as I can, while still having fun in the process.

I am just a student. By no means am I an interpreter or an ASL teacher, and this book is not a manual to start learning ASL, nor is it an educational book of any kind. I think some of the humor here stems from the fact that these are "everyday" American-English slang phrases that I'm translating into ASL. The phrases themselves are funny and outrageous, and seeing them in sign language just gives them another angle for how ridiculous they are. In addition, as these phrases can be somewhat vulgar, I would not recommend signing them to someone you've just met. If you've just met another English speaker, you're not going to randomly tell them "I want to tongue punch your fart box," and adding in a difference of language and culture doesn't make that any less vulgar or offensive.

I started writing this book because I wanted to share how awesome and exciting it is to start learning ASL. As with learning any new language, I was initially interested in finding out how to sign the dirty words. This sparked an interest in me to learn the rest of the language as well, and I've really enjoyed my journey in learning about ASL and Deaf culture. If you'd like to start learning how to sign, I would highly recommend it, as you can obviously have a great time doing so.

I hope this book will spark an interest in you to learn more about ASL, and start your own journey into Deaf culture. Enjoy!

Super Smutty
SIGN LANGUAGE

Chapter 1

THE SEVEN WORDS YOU CAN'T SAY ON TELEVISION

In most beginner language classes, you learn some of the most commonly used words like "book" and "door." Not me! I set out to learn the dirtiest words first. Comedian George Carlin famously talked about the seven words you're not allowed to say on television, so I think those would be great to define as the most basic words of smut. Let's get started!

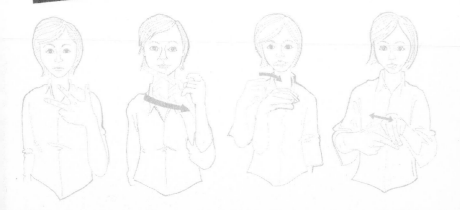

SHIT

PISS

FUCK

3

COCK

CUNT

MOTHERFUCKER

4

TITS

Chapter 2

SWEARING 101

Seven words can only get you so far. If you want to go a little further with what you need to describe, it helps to know a few more simple words that can get your point across. I tried to include a whole array of different slang in this chapter, so if you're not sure what a term means, I recommend Urban Dictionary.

GODDAMN

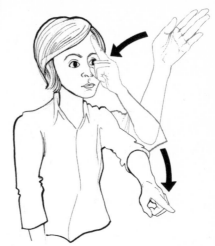

BITCH

BASTARD

KNOW: This is the same sign as "bitch," but is signed at the upper part of the face, which is for masculine signs.

BONER

FART

69

BULLSHIT

HAIR

VAGINA

HAIR CLASSIFIER

11

STRIPPER

NAKED

PERSON

12

BUTTER FACE

WOMAN

SHAPELY BODY

FACE

REALLY UGLY

KNOW: Your mouth should be in the shape of an upside-down U during "really ugly."

FLIRT

TEXTING

ABOUT

FUCK

14

COCKBLOCK

 **FUCK**

 **EFFORT**

 **WOMAN**

 **INTRUDE**

15

FUCKTARD

FUCK

RETARD

SHARK WEEK

 SHARK

 WEEK

 WHAT

MENSTRUATION

GAYDAR

GAY

NOTICE

DUMBASS

 STUPID

 A

 S

 S

19

DOUCHEBAG

WATER

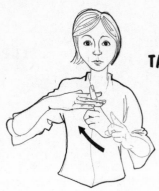

TAMPON

SQUEEZE UNDER TAMPON

DICKWAD

 DICK

 W

 A

 D

 STUPID

CALL

FUCK

WANT

CUM DUMPSTER

WOMAN

CUM DIRECTIONAL

KISS-FIST

KNOW:

"Kiss-fist" is an ASL idiom meaning "I love that" or "that's so good."

JESUS TITTY-FUCKING CHRIST

JESUS

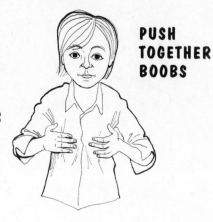

PUSH
TOGETHER
BOOBS

DICK UP
BOOBS

CHRIST

BROWN STAR

BROWN

STAR

MEAN

ASSHOLE

25

DOUCHE CANOE

 WATER

 TAMPON

 SQUEEZE
UNDER
TAMPON

  CANOE

BIG OLD TITTIES

BIG BOOBS

KNOW: Think of the motion of how boobs jiggle. The slower you sign this, the bigger the boobs.

MILF

 MOTHER

 I

 FUCK

 WANT

28

SUGAR TITS

SWEET

BOOBS

TRAMP STAMP

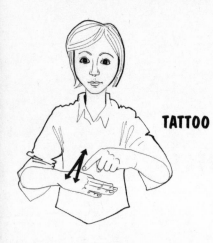

TATTOO

FOR

SLUT

BLUE BALLS

TESTICLES

HURT

FUCK

WANT

TWAT WAFFLE

PUSSY

HOORAY!

I wouldn't recommend looking up "blue waffle" though.

WAFFLE

COCKTEASE

 WOMAN

 FLIRT

 FUCK

 WANT

 TOO BAD

CRUSTY PANTIES

UNDERWEAR

DIRTY

OLD

SHART

 POOP

 FART

 SAME TIME

TWAT

PUSSY

BEARDED CLAM

VAGINA

HAIR

BEARD CLASSIFIER

PUSSY

LABIA MAJORA

CAMEL TOE

 VAGINA

 INSIDE

 PANTS

 SUCKED IN

HOORAY!

Feel free to emphasize
the last sign to say
"moose knuckle."

39

BEEF CURTAINS

BEEF

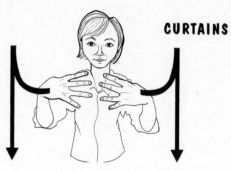

CURTAINS

MEAN

PUSSY

LABIA MAJORA

MASTURBATION

MASTURBATE (GUY)

MASTURBATE (GIRL)

GOLDEN SHOWER

PENIS

SHOWER

THE SHOCKER
(two in the pink, one in the stink)

 SHOCKER

 VAGINA

 VAGINA
WITH
ANUS

 SHOCKER
ON VAGINA
WITH ANUS

BLUMPKIN

 BLOWJOB

 POOP

 SAME TIME

DONKEY PUNCH

 **DONKEY**

 **PUNCH**

 **MEAN**

 **ANAL SEX**

 **PULL OUT**

 **HEAD CLASSIFIER**

 **PUNCH HEAD**

DIRTY SANCHEZ

 ANAL SEX

 PULL OUT

 YOUR

 FACE

 DICK
WIPE
ACROSS

RUSTY TROMBONE

 MASTURBATE (GUY)

 LICK ANUS

 SAME TIME

BONDAGE

BONDAGE

KNOW:

You should have some slight shoulder movement. Facial expression should show a furrowed brow and a tight mouth to show this is hard work.

CHOKING THE CHICKEN

 **CHOKE**

 **CHICKEN**

 **MEAN**

 **MASTURBATE (GUY)**

KNOW: Puff your cheeks out during "choke."

PEARL NECKLACE

PEARL

MEAN

SEMEN
CLASSIFIER

RIMJOB

LICK ANUS

BROS BEFORE HOS

 FRIEND

 SWEETHEART

 HE

 IMPORTANT

Chapter 3

TIME TO FLIRT

What if you see a sexy lady and want to show her how multilingual you are? Or what if the bar is really noisy, but you still want to use your best pick-up line? I'm here to help! Sign language is really great if you need to communicate in a loud environment or from a distance. And if you're relaying a message as important as "I like your boobies," shouldn't you know how to say it in as many languages as possible?

HOW BIG IS YOUR DICK?

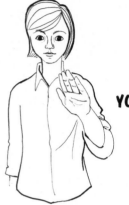 YOUR

 PENIS

 BIG

KNOW: Lean in slightly and hold the last sign, since this is a question.

55

ARE YOU DTF?

YOU

FUCK

READY
QUESTIONING

Now you can sign along with the cast of *Jersey Shore*.

56

BREAK ME OFF A PIECE OF THAT!

 PERSON

 THAT

 WOW

 WANT

KNOW:

The third sign is an idiom in ASL meaning "odd" or "whoa" with the implication that something really out of the ordinary happened, like you saw a plane crash, or a super sexy lady walked by.

NICE SHOES, WANNA FUCK?

 **FANCY**

 **SHOES**

 **WANT**

 **FUCK**

KNOW: The first sign is really versatile. It can mean "cool," "neat," "impressive," etc.

I LIKE YOUR BOOBIES!

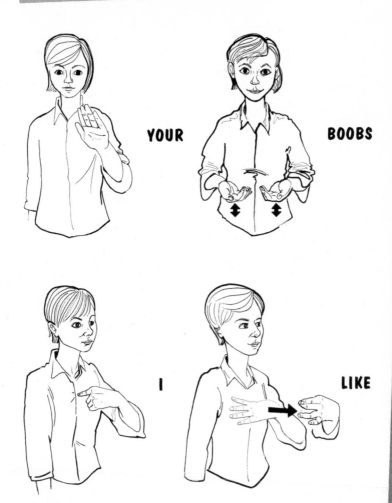

YOUR

BOOBS

I

LIKE

I LOST MY VIRGINITY, CAN I HAVE YOURS?

 MY

 VIRGIN

 FINISH

 YOUR

 VIRGIN

 WANT

NICE ASS!

 YOUR

 BUTT

 SHAPELY BUTT

KNOW: You can have fun with the last sign to make whatever shape you think is sexy.

I WANT TO MOTORBOAT YOUR BOOBS

 YOUR

 BOOBS

 I

 MOTORBOAT

I'M DRUNK, CAN I GO HOME WITH YOU?

I

DRUNK

YOUR

HOUSE

GO

DON'T MIND

KNOW:

Raise your eyebrows during "don't mind," since you're asking a question.

63

YOU WANT TO TOUCH IT?

 TOUCH

 TOUCH HERE

 WANT

KNOW: The "touch here" hand can go wherever. Remember to raise your eyebrows at the end.

SO HOT, WANT TO TOUCH THE HINEY!

 YOU

 WOW

 TOUCH

 BUTT

 WANT

MY DICK IS, LIKE, SUPER-SIZED

MY

COCK

COCK
HANGS
DOWN

I THINK ABOUT YOU WHEN I MASTURBATE

I

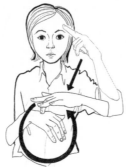

OBSESS

YOU

MASTURBATE
(GUY)

KNOW:

During "obsess," you should move your tongue back and forth, like you're French-kissing the air.

WHO WANTS MY FISH TACO?

MY

FISH

TACO

WANT

WHO

THERE'S A PARTY IN MY PANTS, AND YOU'RE INVITED

 MY

 PANTS

 PARTY

 YOU

 WELCOME

HOORAY!

Pants parties are always fun!

YOUR PLACE OR MINE?

 YOUR

 HOUSE

 MY

 HOUSE

 FUCK

 WHICH

KNOW: This phrase has two options, so make sure to shift your body weight between "your house" and "my house."

I WANT TO EAT YOUR LESBIAN VAGINA

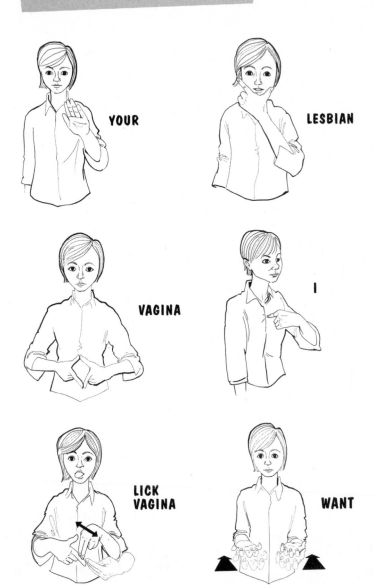

YOUR

LESBIAN

VAGINA

I

LICK
VAGINA

WANT

I WANT TO SUCK YOUR GAY COCK

 YOUR

 GAY

 BONER

 I

 BLOWJOB

 WANT

YOU HAVE NICE DSLs

 YOUR

 LIPS

 GOOD

 FOR

 BLOWJOB

KNOW: The sign for "lips" is similar to the sign for "mouth" but make sure to move your finger around your lips, instead of the general area of your mouth.

BOOBS

FANCY

HOW MUCH FOR A BLOWJOB?

YOU

BLOWJOB

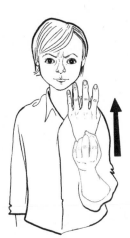

HOW MUCH?

KNOW:

Raise your eyebrows during "blowjob" since you're asking for one.

75

WANT TO GO OVER THERE AND FUCK?

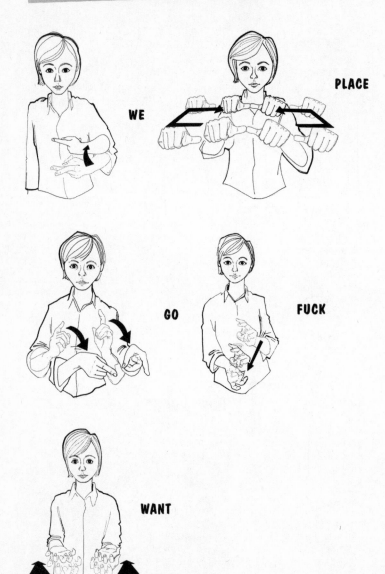

WE

PLACE

GO

FUCK

WANT

WILL YOU TOSS MY SALAD?

 MY

 SALAD

 YOU

 TOSS SALAD IN AIR

 MEAN

 LICK ANUS

KNOW: Remember to puff your cheeks out during "salad."

77

DOES THE CARPET MATCH THE CURTAINS?

 YOUR

 HAIR

 YOUR

 VAGINA

 HAIR CLASSIFIER

 COLOR

 SAME

KNOW:

"Same" can be a directional sign, so we're using it here between upper hair and lower hair.

78

WANT TO PLAY LEAPFROG NAKED?

 **WE**

 **NAKED**

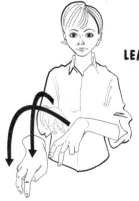 **LEAPFROG**

 **PLAY**

WANT

HOORAY!

This is a lot more fun than naked Twister.

79

YOU'RE A FOXY LADY!

 YOU

 WOMAN

 FOX

 MEAN

 SHAPELY BODY

 WOW

I'M SMALL BUT MIGHTY

 MY

 PENIS

 TINY ERECTION

 BUT

 STRONG

I'M SMALL BUT I TRY

 MY

 PENIS

 TINY ERECTION

 BUT

 EFFORT

KNOW: Make sure to furrow your brow during "effort" to show emphasis.

82

I'D TAP THAT

 **THAT**

 **FUCK**

 **CAN**

WHO WANTS A MUSTACHE RIDE?

 MUSTACHE

 RIDE

 WANT

 WHO

KNOW: Sign "ride" near your mouth for emphasis.

84

I WANT TO FUCK YOUR HAIR

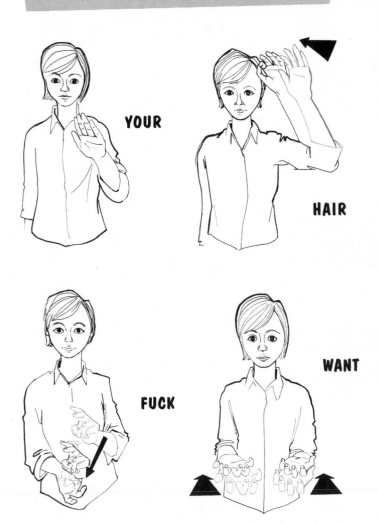

YOUR

HAIR

FUCK

WANT

85

I WANT TO WAKE UP IN YOUR LEGS

 YOUR

 SPREAD LEGS

 HEAD CLASSIFIER

 PUT HEAD BETWEEN LEGS

 WAKE UP

 WANT

EXPECT A DRUNK DIAL SOON

 I

 DRUNK

 SOON

 CALL

 WILL

WE NEED A THIRD

 IF

 WE

 FUCK

 THIRD

 NEED

YOU'RE BETTER THAN PORN

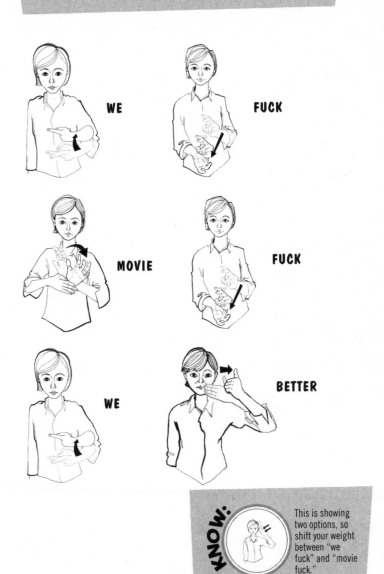

WE

FUCK

MOVIE

FUCK

WE

BETTER

KNOW: This is showing two options, so shift your weight between "we fuck" and "movie fuck."

I JUST GOT LAID

 **RECENTLY**

 **I**

 **FUCK**

 **FINISH**

HOLY JESUS, I WANT TO LICK THEM

 JESUS

 YES

 YOUR

 BOOBS

 LICK BOOBS

 WANT

KNOW:

Nod during "want" at the end.

I WANT TO BE YOUR SEX SLAVE

 WE

 FUCK

 I

 SLAVE

 FOR

 YOU

HOORAY!

Don't forget to designate a safe word!

I WANT TO EAT YOUR FIRE CROTCH

 YOUR

 VAGINA

 HAIR

RED

 LICK VAGINA

 WANT

SIT ON MY FACE SO I CAN PERFORM CUNNILINGUS

MY

FACE

HEAD CLASSIFIER

SIT ON HEAD

WHY

LICK VAGINA

I WANT TO FUCK YOU IN THE MOUTH

 YOUR

 MOUTH

 I

 BLOWJOB DIRECTIONAL

 PULL HEAD TOWARD HIPS

DO I MAKE YOU WANT TO CREAM YOUR PANTIES?

 YOU

 LOOK AT ME

 HAPPEN

 YOU

 FEMALE ORGASM

 QUESTION

SHUT UP AND SUCK IT ALREADY

 **SHUT UP**

 **NOW**

 **BLOWJOB**

 **NOW**

LESS TALK, MORE ANAL

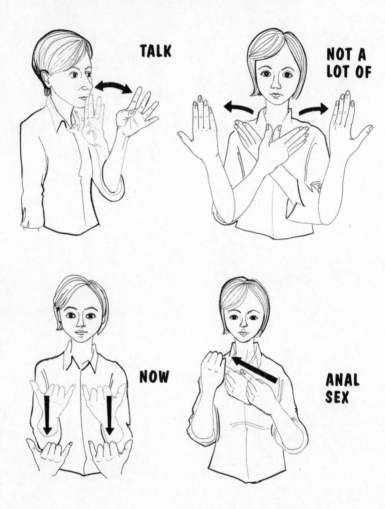

TALK

NOT A LOT OF

NOW

ANAL SEX

GARGLE MY BALLS

 MY

 TESTICLES

 YOU

 SWALLOW

 GARGLE

KNOW:

Make a swishing motion with your cheeks during "gargle."

PLEASE SHAVE YOUR PUBES, I DON'T LIKE FLOSSING

YOUR

VAGINA

HAIR

SHAVE VAGINA

WHY

PULL HAIR FROM TEETH

DON'T

WANT

KNOW:

This use of "why" is rhetorical, so make sure your eyebrows go up instead of down.

WAS THAT A QUEEF?

YOU

PUSSY

PUSSY FART

QUESTION

DON'T GET ANY JIZZ ON THE COUCH

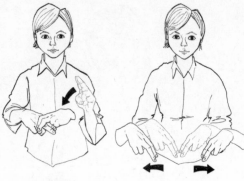

COUCH

YOU

CUM ON
COUCH

NOT ALLOWED

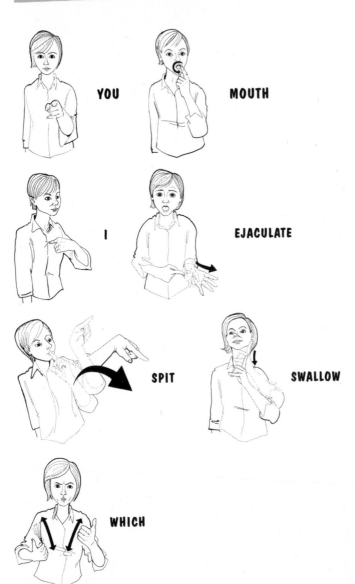

YOU

MOUTH

I

EJACULATE

SPIT

SWALLOW

WHICH

JUST THE TIP, NO TEETH

 MY

 PENIS

 JUST THE TIP

 TEETH

 BITE

 NOT ALLOWED

USE A CONDOM

CONDOM

NEED

HOORAY!

Safe sex is really hot!

BUT I POOP FROM THERE!

 YOU

 ANAL SEX

 WANT

 KNOW THAT

 POOP

 POINT TO ANUS

 QUESTION

DO YOU LIKE ROPE BONDAGE?

 YOU

 BONDAGE

 WITH

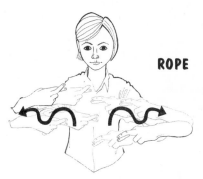 ROPE

 ENJOY

YOU

CAN YOU TIE ME UP?

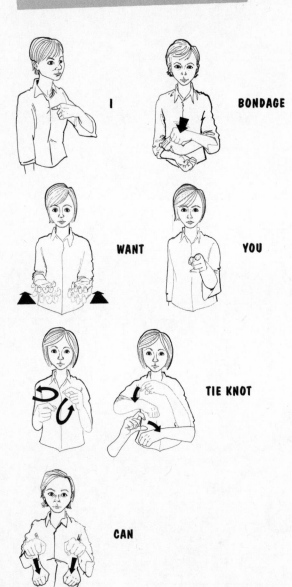

I

BONDAGE

WANT

YOU

TIE KNOT

CAN

I WANT YOU TO LICK IT

 MY

 PENIS

 YOU

 LICK PENIS

 I

 WANT

YOU TASTE GOOD

YOU

TASTE

DELICIOUS

KNOW: When signing "delicious," your mouth should make a shape like you're slurping spaghetti.

BACK THAT ASS UP

 YOUR

 BUTT

 BACK UP

SPANK ME

 NOW  YOU

 SPANK

IS IT IN YET?

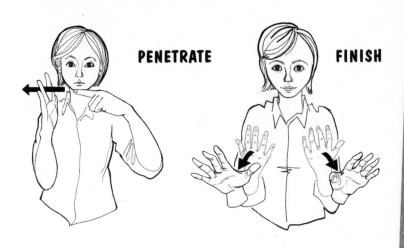

PENETRATE

FINISH

QUESTION

BE QUICK, I HAVE A HEADACHE

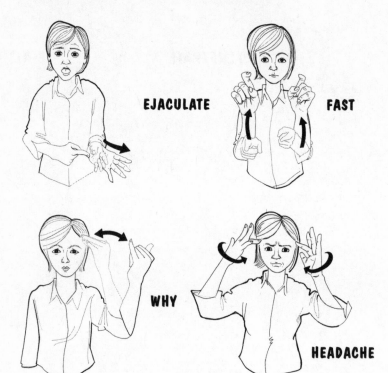

EJACULATE

FAST

WHY

HEADACHE

KNOW: Raise your eyebrows during "ejaculate," since this is the topic of the sentence.

DON'T STOP, HARDER!

KEEP GOING

HARD

115

LOOK HONEY—HANDCUFFS!

 HEY

 SWEETHEART

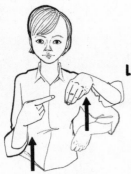 LIFT UP

 C

 CUFFS

IS THAT GONORRHEA?

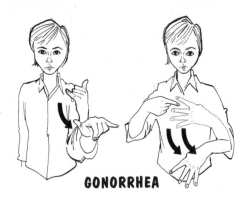

GONORRHEA

THAT

QUESTION

KNOW: Raise your eyebrows during "that," since this is a yes/no question.

I LOVE THE SMELL OF QUEEF IN THE MORNING

 MORNING

I

 PUSSY FART

 SMELL

 KISS-FIST

KNOW:

"Kiss-fist" is an ASL idiom for non-romantic love.

I WANT TO EAT YOUR ANUS

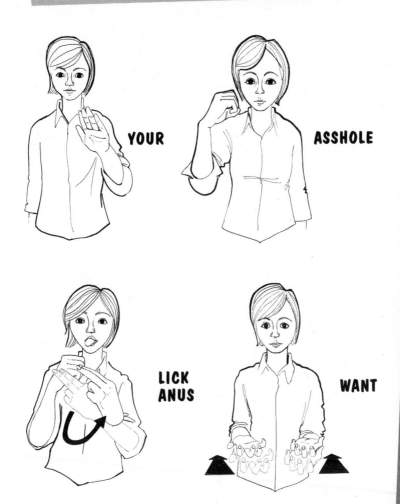

YOUR

ASSHOLE

LICK
ANUS

WANT

MY COCK IS THICK AND VEINY

 MY

 BONER

VEIN
CLASSIFIER

I'M OKAY WITH PERIOD SEX

 WE

 FUCK

 I

 MENSTRUATION

 SAME TIME

 ALLOW

KNOW: Shift your body weight from one side to the other between "we fuck" and "I menstruate." Nod your head when signing "allow."

121

I KNOW A GREAT PLACE TO DRY HUMP

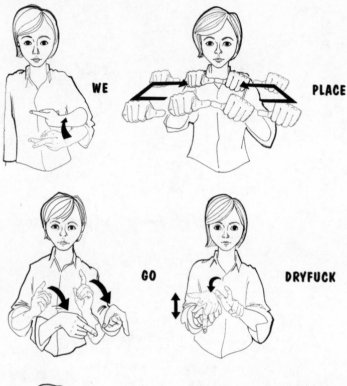

WE

PLACE

GO

DRYFUCK

PERFECT

KNOW:

The sign for "perfect" comes down once and bounces slightly.

I CAUGHT YOU STARING AT MY PACKAGE

 MY

 COCK

 YOU

 LOOK AT ME

 I

 SPOT YOU

I WANT TO MUSHROOM STAMP YOUR FACE

 MY

 PENIS

 YOUR

 HEAD CLASSIFIER

 SMACK FACE

KNOW:

After signing "smack face," you can even pull the penis hand's index finger back and let it "smack the face" again.

I NEED A MORNING AFTER PILL

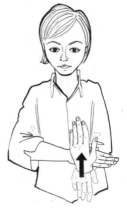

MORNING

AFTER

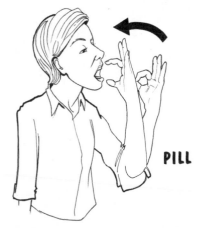

PILL

NEED

WHERE DID YOU PUT THE DILDOES?

 FAKE

 PENIS

 YOU

 HIDE

 WHERE

I'M TOO HORNY TO BE IN PUBLIC

I

HORNY

OUTDOORS

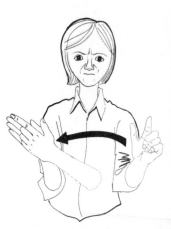

NOT ALLOWED

Chapter 4

INSULTS AND ANGRY PHRASES

Sometimes, an insult just isn't as mean as you need it to be, and you need to say it in another language to really drive home how stupid the other person is. I've included a whole range of insults here, including everything from calling out someone on the smell of their fecal matter to the size of their penis.

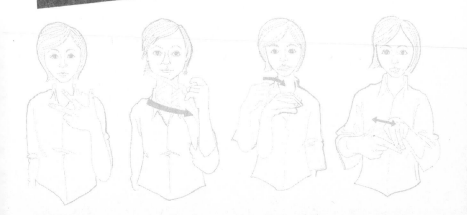

YOUR POOP STINKS!

 YOUR

 POOP

 SMELL

 AWFUL

KNOW:

Your mouth should be in the shape of an upside-down U during the sign for "awful."

DIE IN A FIRE

 YOU

 DEAD

 HOW

 FIRE

HOORAY!

Build a man a fire and he'll be warm for a day, but set a man on fire and he'll be warm for the rest of his life.

YOUR MOM'S A FILTHY WHORE

 YOUR

 MOTHER

 WHORE

 DIRTY

133

FUCK THAT SHIT

FUCK IT

KNOW: Make sure you have a negative facial expression with your eyebrows and mouth.

CUNT WHORE!

CUNT

WHORE

KNOW: Fingerspelling "cunt" would also work, but I think this sign gets the meaning across.

135

GO SUCK YOUR MOM'S DICK

 YOUR

 MOTHER

 COCK

 YOU

 BLOWJOB

136

WHY

EVERY NIGHT

YOU

MASTURBATE (GUY)

YOU NEED A HIGH-FIVE IN THE FACE WITH A CHAIR

 YOUR

 FACE

 HEAD CLASSIFIER

 CHAIR

 CHAIR SMASHES FACE

 NEED

YOU MAKE BABY JESUS CRY

 BABY

 JESUS

 CRIES

 WHY

FORMAL YOU

KNOW: This is a more formal sign for "you," taken to mean "all of this right here."

139

BLOW ME

BLOWJOB

140

SUCK A BAG OF DICKS

 **BAG**

 **INSIDE**

 **DICK**

 **MANY**

 **DICKS IN BAG**

 **LOTS OF BLOWJOBS**

This might be the strangest insult ever!

BITCH, PLEASE!

BITCH

FINISH

142

GO FUCK YOURSELF

FUCK

YOURSELF

YOU CUM-GUZZLING ASS PIRATE!

YOU

CUM
DIRECTIONAL

SWALLOW

BUTT

PIRATE

144

YOU SUCK BALLS

YOU

TESTICLES

SUCK BALLS

KNOW: Make sure to keep your mouth open and move your tongue around during "suck balls."

145

STFU

SHUT UP

FUCK YOU

KNOW:

The closed hand from "shut up" rolls over and into the middle finger for "fuck you."

YOUR WIFE HAS A LOOSE ANUS

 YOUR

 WIFE

 ASSHOLE

 LOOSE

YOUR MOMMA'S SO STUPID

 YOUR

 MOTHER

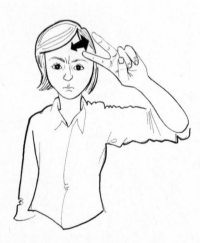 STUPID

GO PLAY "HIDE AND GO FUCK YOURSELF"!

YOU

PLAY

WHAT

HIDE

FUCK

YOURSELF

PANTY SNIFFER

UNDERWEAR

SMELL

PERSON

YOU LOOKED BETTER WHEN I WAS DRUNK

HAPPEN

I

DRUNK

YOU

PRETTY

NOW

REALLY UGLY

YOU STUPID SON OF A BITCH!

YOU

STUPID

S

B

KNOW: The "s" hand comes forward to make the "b."

I KNOW A HO WHEN I SEE ONE

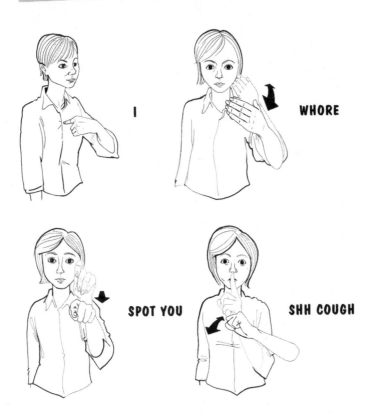

I

WHORE

SPOT YOU

SHH COUGH

KNOW:

The last sign is an ASL idiom that can be taken to mean "I know what I'm doing" or "That's easy for me."

153

SPERM BURPER

YOU

BURP

SPERM

TWAT FACE

 YOUR

 FACE

 PUSSY

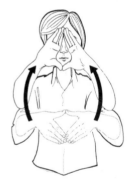 PUSSY UP TO FACE

 LOOK LIKE

155

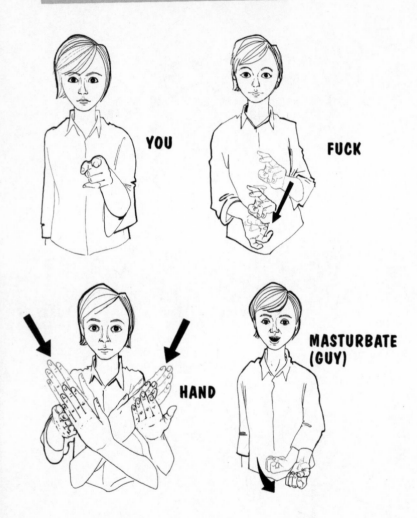

YOU

FUCK

HAND

MASTURBATE
(GUY)

HAVE A NICE CUP OF SHUT THE FUCK UP!

 CUP

 INSIDE

 SHUT UP

 FUCK YOU

 PUT
FUCK YOU
IN CUP

 GIVE
CUP

HEY! DID YOU JUST CALL ME A CUNT?!

 HEY

 YOU

 LABEL

 PUSSY

KNOW: This is a yes/no question, so raise your eyebrows at the end.

YOUR DADDY DRINKS
BECAUSE YOU CRY

YOUR

FATHER

DRUNK

PERSON

WHY

YOU

CRIES

GO PLAY IN TRAFFIC

 TRAFFIC

 YOU

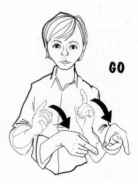 GO

PLAY

PLAY

THERE

KNOW:

In the sign for "there," you're pointing to the spot where you signed "traffic" earlier.

NOBODY LIKES YOU

PEOPLE

LIKE

YOU

NONE

BLOW IT OUT YOUR ASS!

YOUR

ASSHOLE

BLOW
THROUGH
WITH
FINGERS

GO PISS UP A TREE

 **PENIS**

 **YOU**

 **TREE**

 **UP TREE**

KNOW:

Shake the hand pointed upward during "up tree" to show urination.

IF I AGREED WITH YOU, WE'D BOTH BE WRONG

 HAPPEN

 WE

 AGREE

 BOTH

 WRONG

KNOW: Nod during "both" and "wrong."

YOUR GIRLFRIEND IS FUGLY

 YOUR

 SWEETHEART

 FUGLY

KNOW: Make sure to make a disgusted "Aw hell no!" face during the last sign.

YOU'RE A SMELLY PIRATE HOOKER!

YOU

PIRATE

WHORE

SMELL

AWFUL

YOU

166

YOU RAT BASTARD

 RAT

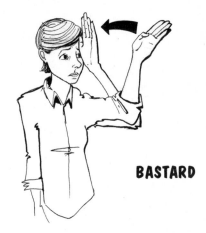 BASTARD

 YOU

YOU'RE HUNG LIKE A HAMSTER

HAMSTER

SMALL

CUTE

YOUR

PENIS

SAME

HOORAY!

Maybe it's a really big hamster?

Chapter 5

POP CULTURE REFERENCES

If you're anything like me and my friends, then you love quoting lines from movies and TV shows to each other. This is even more fun if the quote is dirty! I've put together a whole bunch of pop culture references from everything from Monty Python to *Anchorman* that are still hilarious in sign language.

YOU MOTORBOATING SON OF A BITCH

 YOU

 BOOBS

 MOTORBOAT

 S

B

 YOU

HOORAY!

She just eye-fucked the shit out of you.

FUCK YOU, YOU FUCKING FUCK!

 **FUCK YOU**

 **YOU**

 **FUCK**

 **F**

 **K**

SOMETIMES IT'S OKAY TO GO ASS TO MOUTH

 SOMETIMES

 ANAL SEX

 TURN AROUND TO BLOWJOB

 BLOWJOB

ALLOW

MY ANUS IS BLEEDING!

MY

ASSHOLE

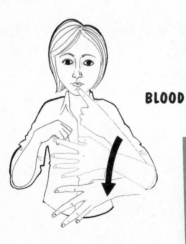

BLOOD

HOORAY!

For the love of God, and all that is holy, my anus is bleeding!

I WANT TO DIP MY BALLS IN IT

 MY

 TESTICLES

 THAT

 DIP CLASSIFIER

 WANT

YOU COCKY COCK!

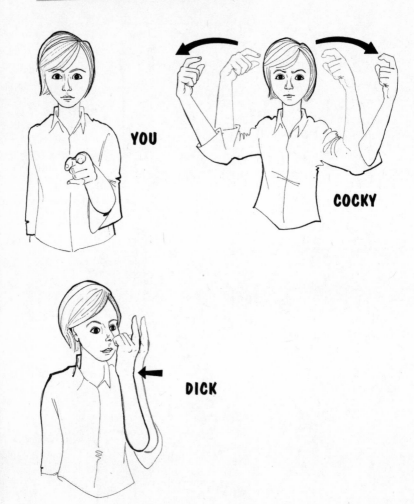

YOU

COCKY

DICK

YOU KNOW HOW I KNOW YOU'RE GAY?

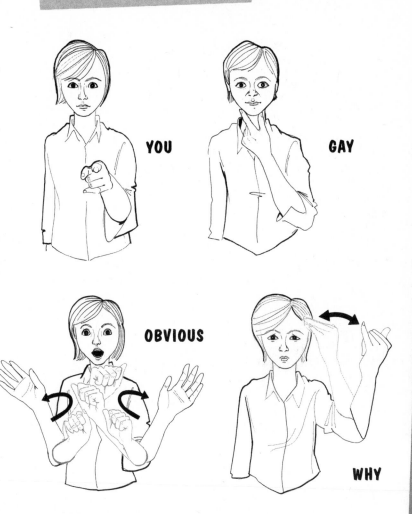

YOU

GAY

OBVIOUS

WHY

I FART IN YOUR GENERAL DIRECTION!

FART

FART WAFTS
TOWARD
PERSON

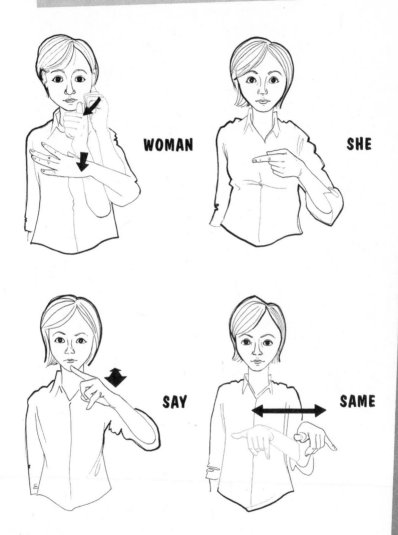

WOMAN

SHE

SAY

SAME

WE

BE ON
YOU
CLOSE

WANT

I HAVE THE WEIRDEST BONER RIGHT NOW

NOW

I

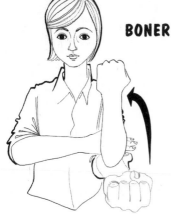

BONER

AWKWARD

POOP

POOP BIRD

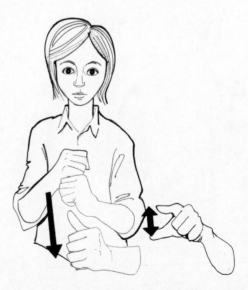

I DARE YOU, I DOUBLE DARE YOU, MOTHERFUCKER!

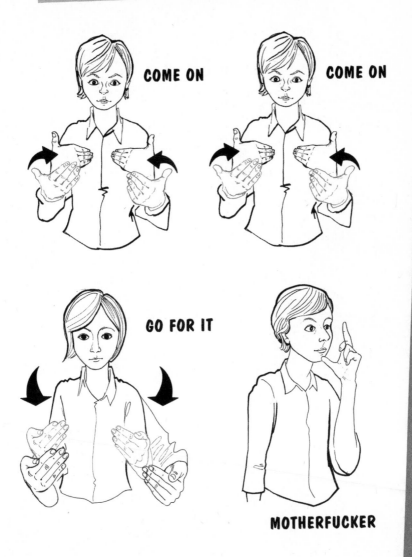

COME ON

COME ON

GO FOR IT

MOTHERFUCKER

SCREW YOU GUYS, I'M GOING HOME

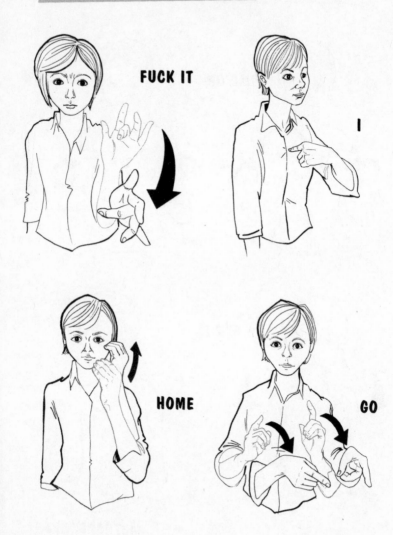

FUCK IT

I

HOME

GO

SHUT YOUR FUCKING FACE, UNCLE FUCKER!

SHUT UP

FUCK YOU

UNCLE

FUCK

PERSON

KNOW: The closed hand from "shut up" rolls over and into the middle finger for "fuck you."

IT TASTES LIKE BURNING!

TASTE

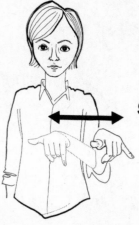

SAME

BURN

KNOW: Puff your cheeks a little during "burn."

COCK-JUGGLING THUNDER CUNT!

 MAN

 THREE

 YOU

 BLOWJOB HANDJOB ON THREE

 SAME TIME

 PUSSY

 BIG FLOBBITY PUSSY

KNOW: You should be saying "Thbbt" with your mouth during the last sign.

187

AMERICA, FUCK YEAH!

AMERICA

UHH YEAH

YES

KNOW:

The second sign here is an ASL idiom that can mean "You know that's right!"

188

WE'RE GOIN' STREAKING!

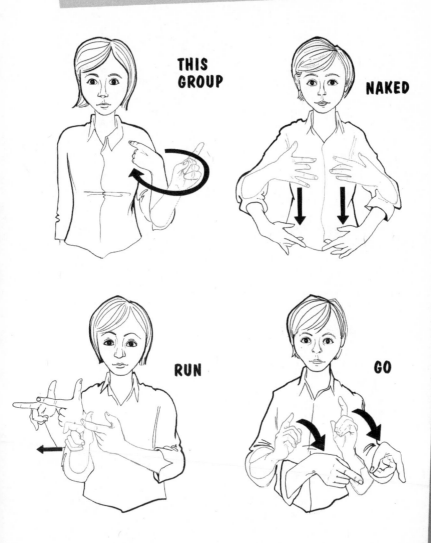

THIS
GROUP

NAKED

RUN

GO

189

THE PRICE IS WRONG, BITCH!

COST

WRONG

BITCH

DOES HE LOOK LIKE A BITCH?

MAN

HE

BITCH

LOOK
LIKE

KNOW:

This is a question, so make sure to raise your eyebrows on "look like."

YOU GOT A PURDY MOUTH

 YOUR

 MOUTH

 FASCINATED

GIANT COCKTOPUS

DICK

BIG

OCTOPUS

COCKTOPUS

KNOW:

Puff your cheeks
out during "big"
and "cocktopus."

HOLLA AT A PLAYER

 I

 PIMP

 WHASSUP

IT'S NO PANTS O'CLOCK!

 NOW

 TIME

 PANTS

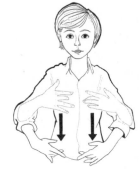 NAKED

 TIME

HOORAY!
No pants dance party!

195

Chapter 6

MORE IMPORTANT PHRASES TO KNOW

This is a miscellaneous chapter for all the other phrases that are still hilarious to learn, but don't necessarily fit in any other category. I hope you enjoy them!

FATTY WANTS CAKE!

CAKE

FAT PERSON

WANT

DON'T DROP THE SOAP

 **SOAP**

 **DROP**

 **DON'T**

KNOW: Make sure to make an upset mouth on "don't."

I HAVE TO TAKE A PISS

I

PENIS

NEED

KNOW:

"Pee" and "penis" are the same sign, but when signing "pee," it's a single quick tap on the nose, whereas the sign for "penis" lingers a bit longer, or it can be a double tap. You can still sign this way if you're a woman.

DON'T TRUST HOS

 **TRUST**

 **WHORE**

 **DON'T**

DON'T EAT THE DEAD LESBIANS, THEY'RE FORBIDDEN

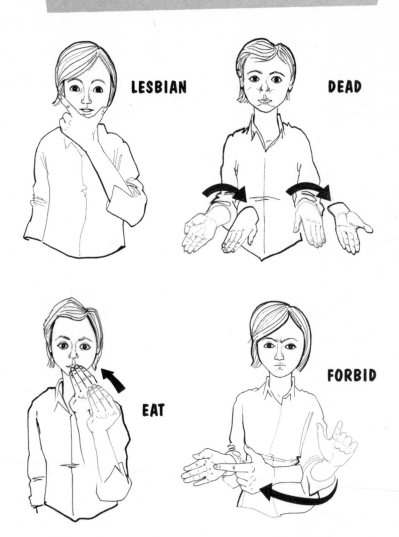

LESBIAN

DEAD

EAT

FORBID

I WILL SHIT IN YOUR MOUTH

 YOUR

 MOUTH

 I

 POOP

 INSIDE

IT'S LIKE JESUS COMING ON YOUR FACE

SAME

YOUR

FACE

JESUS

CUM
DIRECTIONAL

I'M GLAD YOU WEREN'T AN ABORTION

YOU

ABORTION

NOT

I

HAPPY

KNOW: Nod your head during "happy."

206

FUCK ME RUNNING

 F

 K

 I

 RUN

AMAZE

KNOW: The last sign is a culturally Deaf variation, meaning "amazing" or "astounding."

FUCK THE POLICE!

POLICE

FUCK IT

SMELL MY FINGER

MY

FINGER
UNDER
NOSE

SMELL
FINGER

GO FOR IT

HOORAY!

Good things happen if
you pull my finger, too!

WHAT THE FUCK IS GOING ON HERE?

WHAT, ALTERNATE VERSION

F

K

HAPPEN

HAPPEN

KNOW:

Furrow your brows during "happen."

DOES THE POPE SHIT IN THE WOODS?

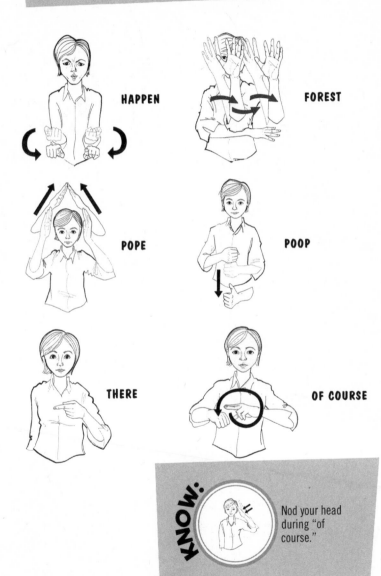

HAPPEN

FOREST

POPE

POOP

THERE

OF COURSE

KNOW:

Nod your head during "of course."

THESE NIPPLES COULD CUT GLASS

ERECT
NIPPLES

GLASS

NIPPLE
CUT
GLASS

212

HERE COME THE MOTHERFUCKING COPS!

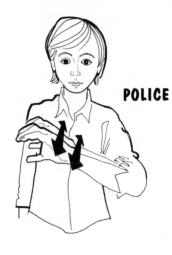

POLICE

MOTHERFUCKER

COME

SOON

FEMINISTS FUCK BETTER

 **WOMAN**

 **PROTEST**

 **PERSON**

 **FUCK**

 **CHAMP**

KNOW: "Champ" is an ASL idiom. It's used when someone's the best at something, like you're crowning a person. The sign comes down once and bounces slightly.

214

DO YOUR BALLS HANG LOW?

 YOUR

 TESTICLES

 LOW

 QUESTION

KNOW: This is a yes/no question, so make sure to raise your eyebrows at the end.

SEE YOU LATER, MASTURBATOR

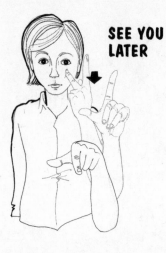

SEE YOU LATER

MASTURBATE (GUY)

PERSON

DON'T BE A SLUT

 SLUT

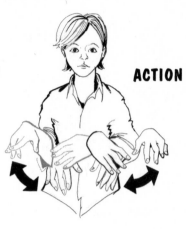 ACTION

 SAME

 DON'T

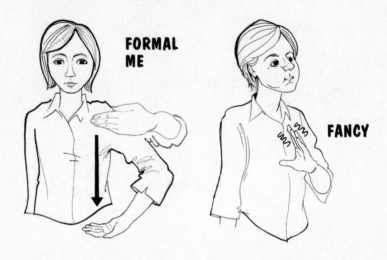

FORMAL
ME

FANCY

MOTHERFUCKER

Chapter 7

SIGNS THAT LOOK SMUTTY BUT AREN'T

Inevitably in any language, there are things that sound or look dirty, but end up being completely innocuous. Here are some signs that really don't mean anything vulgar, but may look pretty bad in the wrong context. Get your mind out of the gutter!

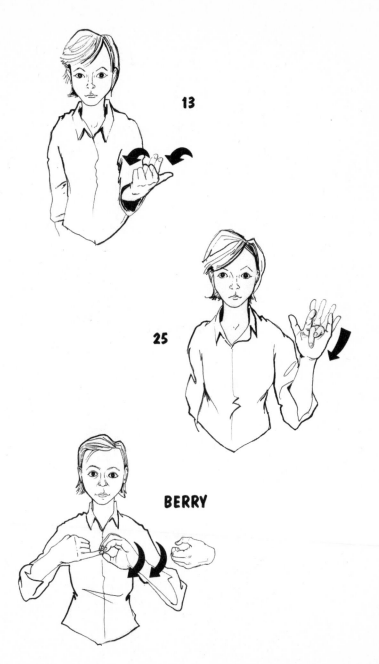

13

25

BERRY

BATTERY

BUTTER

CARROT

CEREAL

CORN

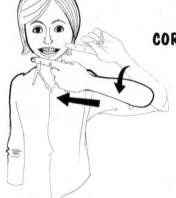

DRAWER

GET DRESSED

MOUTH

PRACTICE

RUSSIA

HOORAY!

The movement in this sign actually comes from the act of wiping vodka off your chin.

SOAP

THUMB DRIVE

225

ASL SIGN LANGUAGE ALPHABET

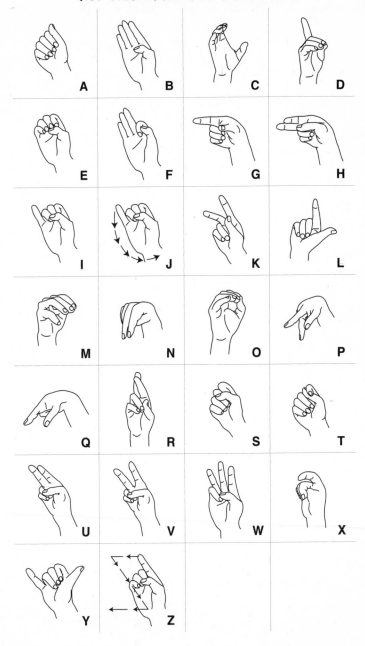

INDEX

Z